THE
JANE
GOODALL
STORY

FOR THE LOVE OF CHIMPS

BY MARTHA E. KENDALL

To the memory of my mother,
Elizabeth Avery Bullen Kendall,
and her mother, Edith Ingersoll Bullen

Front cover photo by Baron Hugo van Lawick.
Courtesy of National Geographic Society.

Published by Worthington Press
801 94th Avenue North, St. Petersburg, Florida 33702

Copyright © 1995 by Worthington Press,
a division of PAGES, Inc.

Printed in the United States of America

2 4 6 8 10 9 7 5 3 1

ISBN 0-87406-779-0

CONTENTS

Photo by Kennan Ward.

Chimps. They are more like humans than any other animal on earth. Protective chimp mothers spend many hours cuddling their pink-faced babies. Rowdy young chimps laugh, chase each other around tree trunks, swing on low branches, and tumble in the dirt. Adult male chimps organize themselves into groups and fight fierce battles to defend their home territory.

In short, chimps act very much like we do! What else do we have in common? How much smarter are we? Can chimps teach us anything about ourselves? For years scientists asked these questions, but there were no good answers. Chimps lived in remote African jungles and ran from people. No one could study them in the wild. No one, that is, until Jane Goodall came along.

At first glance, Jane seems an unlikely person to unlock mysteries about wild chimps. She came to Africa as a young, soft-spoken English woman with no formal training in animal study. But she surprised the world by spending years in the jungle until chimps accepted her as if she were one of them. That acceptance allowed Jane to discover what these wonderful animals are really like.

Today Jane Goodall is one of the most famous scientists in the world. Her work in the field tells us a great deal about the chimps she knows and loves. Her life shows us that a brave, determined person can accomplish amazing things. This is her story.

Photo by Baron Hugo van Lawick.
Courtesy of National Geographic Society.

CHAPTER 1

DAVID GRAYBEARD

In spite of the heavy downpour, Jane walked easily through the thick African forest. She liked the rain.

Suddenly, right in front of her stood a big male chimp, hunched and threatening. Jane froze. The chimp was only about four feet tall, but Jane knew that he had the strength of three grown men. She heard a sound above her. A large chimp stared down at her from a vine. He gave a loud, spine-tingling screech, a sound chimps use to threaten a dangerous animal. Another chimp only a few yards away glared and shook a big branch at Jane, sending a shower of rain, twigs, and leaves onto her head. From behind, another chimp let out a long, savage wail.

Jane was surrounded.

Running away was out of the question. Chimps can easily outrun a person. Jane crouched low, wanting the chimps to believe she was no threat. Her heart pounding, she tried to stay still, hoping not to be attacked. After a few minutes of silence, Jane pretended to ignore the chimps and acted as if she were eating roots that she slowly picked up from the ground.

Then the male in front of her charged! He ran straight toward her, his black hair bristling with rage. The moment before he reached her, he swerved. Two more chimps charged, but neither of them touched her. And then, as quickly as they had come, the chimps disappeared into the dense forest. Jane waited until all she could hear were the raindrops falling around her. She stood up, her legs trembling. Weighing only ninety pounds, she would have had no chance if the chimps had attacked.

Jane did not dwell much on the danger she had just

escaped. After all, she did not come to Africa to avoid danger. Ever since she was a little girl growing up in England, she had wanted to live among wild animals, and at last her dream had come true. For months, she had been spending every day searching the jungle for chimps. She wanted to learn as much about them as she could.

Jane realized that her daily presence in the jungle was making the chimps so curious about her that they were overcoming their fear of humans. The male chimps had charged within inches of her. But instead of thinking about what might have happened if they had attacked, Jane thought about David Graybeard. She believed that if he had been there, the chimps would have acted differently.

David Graybeard was the first chimp to visit her camp on the shore of Lake Tanganyika (Tan-gan-YEE-ka). Jane had been living there for nearly a year. The white hair on his chin made him easy to recognize, so Jane named him David Graybeard. He first approached the camp to eat the fruit of the oil-nut palms that grew near the tents. Jane was not at camp at the time of his visit, because she was searching the forest for chimps.

But Dominic, the cook, watched David feed on the fruit and help himself to bananas intended for Jane's dinner.

Jane was thrilled by the news of David's visit. Although other chimps she spotted from a distance ran away terrified at the sight of a person, David dared even to enter the camp. Human smells, tents, tables, chairs, and supplies did not frighten him off. Jane told Dominic to leave more bananas out just in case David came again. The next day Jane returned to the forest, and David returned to camp! Not wanting to miss him again, Jane waited in camp to see if he would come another time. He did. He became a regular visitor, growing so comfortable around Jane that one time he actually took a banana from her hand.

But Jane and David Graybeard did not spend all day in camp. When Jane saw him in the forest, he sometimes came right up to her to see if she had a banana hidden in her pocket. Other chimps watched with fascination. From David Graybeard's calm example, some of them slowly grew less fearful of the strange human creature who had entered their world.

The group of male chimps who charged Jane during

Photo by Baron Hugo van Lawick. Courtesy of National Geographic Society.

Jane and David Graybeard share a banana snack on a jungle trail.

the rainstorm did not accept her yet. But she was pleased that they had come close, without harming her. Jane hoped all the chimps in the area would gradually become so used to her that they would ignore her. She promised herself never to betray their trust.

Jane had David Graybeard to thank for two of her most exciting early discoveries about chimpanzees. One morning she spotted him sitting on a termite mound. He picked a blade of grass, poked it into a tunnel in the mound, and then pulled it out. Clinging to the grass were termites galore—a delicious feast for a chimp. Again and again, David "fished" for termites using his blade of grass.

Jane returned to the termite mound day after day, hoping to observe more. On the eighth day she saw David Graybeard along with another chimp whom she named Goliath. She watched the chimps use their thumbs and forefingers to scratch open the entrances to the termites' tunnels. Then they inserted their tools. If a twig broke or was bent, they made another "fishing pole" by finding a twig and pulling the leaves off it. Sometimes they made several at a time, stacking them

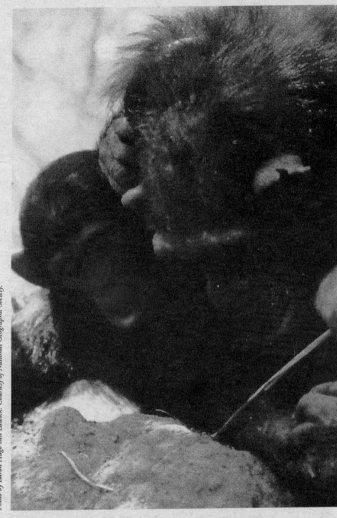

Photo by Baron Hugo van Lawick. Courtesy of National Geographic Society.

One of Jane Goodall's most exciting discoveries was that chimpanzees—like humans—make and use tools. Here a young chimp watches as his mother uses a blade of grass to fish termites from a mound.

nearby to be available when needed. Jane realized that chimps actually make tools and plan ahead to use them. She was thrilled to be the first person to see this intelligent behavior of chimps in the wild. Scientists had long thought that one of the biggest differences between humans and animals was that only humans could make and use tools. Jane's observation showed that chimpanzees could, too.

Jane discovered something else new about chimpanzees. She saw David Graybeard eating a piglet. Two other chimps, a female and a youngster, reached out their hands. David allowed them to take pieces of the meat right from his mouth. Scientists knew chimps might occasionally eat insects or small rodents, but they thought chimps did not eat larger animals. Now Jane knew they did.

Jane sent telegrams about her observations to Dr. Louis Leakey, who was as excited as she was about the discoveries. He was the famous curator (or director) of what is now the National Museum of Natural History in Kenya. He searched for clues about the first humans. He encouraged Jane to study chimps, the most humanlike animals in the world. After receiving Jane's telegram about her discoveries, he used his influence to get more money so she could continue her research.

Jane could not have been happier. To live among the wild animals in Africa had been her goal ever since she was a little girl, and now she was fulfilling her dream.

CHAPTER 2

JUBILEE AND THE DREAM

Even as a baby Jane was very sensitive to the natural world around her. One afternoon her grandmother parked Jane's baby carriage in the yard so Jane could enjoy the sunshine and fresh air. A dragonfly darted past Jane's face. Its wings sparkled, and Jane was fascinated by their bright, fluttering movement. When the milkman came by, he teased, "Watch out for the dragonfly's tail because it can sting." (Actually, a dragonfly cannot sting, but the milkman may have thought it could simply because its tail is so long.) A short while later, Jane's grandmother pushed the baby carriage into town. She left the carriage outside a shop while she ran in to buy a magazine. Another dragonfly flew by. Once again Jane was entranced by its motion. When the dragonfly dipped near her face, Jane moved away from the tail. A man who happened to pass by used his folded newspaper to swat the dragonfly away from her. It dropped into the baby carriage.

The dragonfly's wings still fluttered in the breeze, but Jane knew it was dead. Upset that the beautiful creature had been killed simply because it had come near her, Jane cried and cried. Jane's grandmother ran outside to see what had happened. Years later she realized that the incident showed that baby Jane already loved all living things.

When Jane was almost two years old, the London Zoo announced that its first chimpanzee infant had been born there. The year was 1935, and England was celebrating King George's twenty-fifth anniversary on the throne. The celebration was called a Silver Jubilee. Souvenirs of the event, such as statues, towels, and hats, were sold everywhere. Because of this celebration, the baby chimp was named Jubilee. After Jubilee was born, stuffed chimps of the same name were found in every gift shop.

Jane's father, Mortimer Goodall, bought a toy chimp for his daughter. Concerned friends told him not to give Jane the lifelike toy. They said it would frighten her and cause nightmares. They warned him that it would have a serious, long-lasting impact on her.

Mortimer and his wife, Vanne, knew their daughter better than their well-meaning friends did. They gave Jane her present, and she loved Jubilee from the moment she saw him. She hugged him, talked to him, dragged him by her side, and held him when she slept. Enjoying sweet dreams, she listened to the melodies played by the music box hidden inside Jubilee's soft body. Her parents' friends turned out to be right about only one thing. Chimps certainly would have a major impact on her.

Jane was curious about all kinds of animals. In fact, when she was just a few years old, she took a handful of worms to bed with her one night. She wanted to see how they walked without legs and to watch how they wiggled

Photo by Nancy Rillstone. Courtesy of the Jane Goodall Institute.

Young Jane cuddles Jubilee, the first "chimp" she ever loved.

on her pillow. When her mother came to kiss Jane good night, she found the dirty pile of worms. She did not scold Jane and throw the worms out the window in disgust. Instead, she said, "Jane, if you leave the worms here, they'll be dead in the morning. They need to live in the earth." Jane quickly gathered up the worms, ran downstairs, and put them back in the garden.

When she was about four, Jane made her first carefully planned, patient study of animals. Her family had moved from London to the large old house where her father had grown up. The house was in the country, and Jane loved the sheep, cows, and pigs on the farm next door. Geese roamed her front yard and hens lived in a large pen. One of her favorite chores was to feed the chickens and collect eggs. But she had a question she couldn't find the answer to: where did the eggs come from? She could not imagine where a hen had an opening large enough for an egg to come out. She decided to follow a hen into the hen house to find out. But the hen was not about to lay an egg after Jane squeezed into the small space next to her. The hen squawked and rushed outside. She obviously considered laying an egg to be her own private business!

Jane needed a new research plan. She decided to go into the empty hen house, hide in the straw at the back, and hope that a hen might come in. She waited and waited. About four hours later, a hen entered. Jane held her breath and tried not to move a muscle. Five feet away on the other side of the hen house, the hen settled down on the straw. She did not notice her young observer. Jane waited some more. At last the hen raised herself up slightly and bent forward. Jane saw a round white object gradually emerge from the feathers between the hen's legs. It got bigger and then dropped onto the straw. Then the hen strutted out of the hen house.

Jane had solved the mystery of where eggs come from! She felt as proud as if she had laid the egg herself. Her eyes shining, and with straw sticking out of her hair and clothes, Jane ran toward the house to share the exciting news with her mother.

By this time, many hours had passed and dusk had fallen. Her mother had grown very worried. Where was Jane? Volunteers had already begun searching for her, trying to reassure Mrs. Goodall that the little girl couldn't have gone very far. Finally the police were called. What a relief when Jane was spotted running down the path, her smiling face lit up with excitement! Instead of punishing Jane for going off without telling her, her mother sat down and listened to her fascinating story about how a hen lays an egg.

When World War II began, Jane's father joined the army. Her mother, Jane, and her younger sister Judy moved in with Jane's grandmother in Bournemouth, a town on the southern coast of England. Her large, red brick house was called the Birches. The family felt relatively safe in Bournemouth, which lay about eighty miles away from war-torn London. Six-year-old Jane played outside and explored the neighborhood. She formed a nature club consisting of herself, her younger sister, and two other girls who spent almost every vacation with Jane's family. It was called the Alligator Club, and Jane was the leader.

The Alligator Club organized many activities. For example, the girls put eight snails in an old wooden box. The box had a glass top so the girls could watch their snails, but it had no bottom. They put the box on leaves in the backyard. Once the snails finished eating the leaves, the girls moved the box to a new spot with more leaves.

The girls decided it would be fun to race their snails. They painted numbers on the shells and placed the snails at the starting line of their racetrack. To keep the snails going straight, the girls touched the sides of the snail's horns with soft pieces of grass. It took a lot of patience to see whose snail would be first to reach the finish line six feet away.

Sometimes at midnight the club members crept outside just for the excitement of being in the familiar backyard at such an unfamiliar hour. The girls loved the moonlight and the cool, moist air. Their only worry was being discovered by the adults, who definitely would not have approved of the children prowling the yard in the middle of the night.

In the afternoons, Jane often took a neighbor's collie with her to the seashore. The beach was only a few minutes' walk from the Birches. Jane worried that the collie did not get enough exercise, so she let him romp and play. Rusty, a spaniel also owned by a neighbor, began to tag along. When Jane tried to teach the collie to shake hands, she was surprised when Rusty was the first to hold out his paw. Jane discovered that Rusty could learn anything she tried to teach him. He could climb a ladder, jump through a hoop, play dead, and toss and catch a biscuit. Unlike most dogs, he liked to be dressed up. Jane put him in an old pair of pajamas and pushed him around in a baby carriage. Rusty's owners did not mind that their dog spent so much time with Jane. It was obvious that Jane and Rusty were very attached to each other.

Rusty liked to please Jane, and he felt guilty if he did something wrong. An easy trick for him was shutting the door on command. One day he did it without being asked. He used his wet, muddy paw, and Jane scolded him for making a mess. He sighed and faced the wall. He sat a few inches from it, staring straight ahead. Jane understood that he was sorry that he had misbehaved. She forgave him, kneeling down and apologizing in a gentle voice.

Jane taught Rusty a great deal, and he taught her, too. She grew to understand him and his ways of learning.

Already in her young life she had years of experience studying animals. Although she did not realize it at the time, she was preparing herself to become the world's most recognized ethologist—a scientist who studies animal behavior.

Jane and her friends went on many nature hikes. Jane wrote down what they saw. When she got home, she looked up the names of the various birds and insects so her notes would be complete. Sometimes the girls climbed down the cliffs to the beach, where they gathered flowers and shells. They collected so many that they decided to display them in their own museum. An uncle let them have a human skeleton that he had owned since he was in medical school, and it became their featured exhibit. The children invited anyone who happened to pass by to come visit their museum. They asked that visitors make a donation to a society for the protection of old horses. The girls gave the society the money that they collected. The society used the money to buy horses who would otherwise have been sent to the slaughterhouse. Thanks to the organization, the horses were sent out to pasture to enjoy their last years grazing in comfort.

Although Jane's family did not own a horse, she did go riding quite often. At a nearby stable, she learned how to groom horses and ponies and how to clean the saddles and bridles. Some mornings she got up at dawn, caught the ponies in the pasture, and rode one back to the stable. She led four or five others with a long rope. As her riding improved, the owners of the stable allowed her to lead trail rides. By the time she was fourteen, she was good enough to enter a horse show and she won ribbons in jumping events.

The one time she went on a fox hunt she loved every minute of it until the very end. It was thrilling to gallop across the English countryside, jump over hedges and stone walls, and listen to the hunting horn and the excited baying of the hounds. But when the fox was caught, Jane felt sick to see the dogs kill it. She never hunted again.

Jane spent some of her happiest moments in her backyard, perched ten feet above the ground. Sitting on the highest branches of the beech tree, she read and dreamed. If she felt angry about something, she would climb the tree and open a book. Soon she forgot her problems and found herself carried to another world.

She read many books about Africa. Her mother got her a library book about Dr. Dolittle, a veterinarian who could talk with all the animals. Jane read the book three times before it had to be returned. For Christmas her grandmother gave Jane her own copy of the book. Jane loved all the Dr. Dolittle stories. Her favorite one was about him taking circus animals back to Africa.

She also read *Tarzan* and grew jealous of Tarzan's jungle friend named Jane. She felt she could have been a far better Jane than the one in the story. She also loved Rudyard Kipling's *The Jungle Book.*

Some afternoons she climbed the beech tree without a book to read. She listened to the birds' songs, watched squirrels and insects, and wrote down what she saw. Sometimes she pictured herself in a forest among the wild animals. Jane decided that someday she would go to Africa.

Her mother knew about Jane's dream. Vanne Goodall's friends said to her, "Why don't you tell Jane to dream about something she can achieve and forget this crazy Africa business?" In those days it was unheard of for a young English girl to enter the African jungle.

But Vanne did not discourage her daughter. She said, "Jane, if you really want to do something, if you work hard enough, if you take advantage of every opportunity, you'll get there in the end if you never give up."

Jane never gave up.

CHAPTER 3

THE LAND OF DR. DOLITTLE

When Jane graduated from high school, she knew that she wanted to work with wild animals. But she had no idea how she could make a living doing that. Jane believed the most practical way to earn money would be as a secretary who could get a job anywhere in the world. She enrolled in a secretarial school in London. However, her first job was not in a faraway place. It was in Bournemouth, where she had grown up. Working at a medical clinic for children, she saw kids who were paralyzed or suffering from deadly diseases. She learned that people with physical limitations did not necessarily have mental ones. Most important, she learned to appreciate her own good health.

By this time her parents had divorced. Jane wanted to study at Oxford University, but her mother could not afford to send her. Jane had earned very good grades in high school, and she tried to win a scholarship. But she did not qualify because she had not mastered a foreign language.

Even though she couldn't attend the university, she wanted to be close to it. She got a job at Oxford and became friends with many students. But she spent some of her most pleasant moments by herself. At dawn and dusk, she often paddled a canoe down the river. She listened to the sound of the flowing water and watched the beautiful swans, ducks, and kingfishers. She also practiced steering a flat-bottomed boat called a punt by pushing off with a long pole. More than once she fell into the river while she struggled to get the knack of it.

In London the next year, she worked during the day at a studio that made documentary films. She spent her spare time in the Natural History Museum. She read more and more books about Africa, never forgetting her childhood dream.

That's when the letter came. Jane's old high school friend Clo had written to invite Jane to visit her and her family at their new farm. The farm was in Kenya, a British colony in East Africa. Jane accepted eagerly. But before she could go, she had to earn the money to pay her way. She enjoyed her job at the London film studio, but it did not pay enough for her to save the amount she needed to travel to Africa. The day she received Clo's letter, she quit her job. She moved back home to Bournemouth and found work as a waitress. Every weekend she put her pay under the carpet. After four months, she pulled back the carpet and counted her money. She had saved enough.

On board the ship to Africa, Jane watched the dolphins, sharks, and flying fish play on the ocean's surface. Sea birds sailed above the waves. During storms, most of the passengers went to their cabins, but Jane climbed to the deck. She never felt seasick. Alone, she stood in awe as the dancing sea tossed the ship up and down.

Jane's journey in 1957 took twenty-one days at sea. After her ship docked in the port of Mombasa in Kenya, she took a train to Nairobi, the capital of Kenya. During most of the two-day train ride, she stared out the window. It took a while for her to fully believe she wasn't watching a movie, but was actually in Africa, seeing real wild animals. At age twenty-three, she arrived at the land of Dr. Dolittle. Clo met Jane in Nairobi. On their way to the farm, Jane got her first close-up look at a giraffe. She marveled at the animal's grace and beauty.

Jane knew it would be bad manners to stay too long as Clo's guest. So before leaving England, she had lined up a secretarial job with a big company that had a branch office in Nairobi. After three wonderful weeks with Clo, Jane started the job. But the office work bored her. She really wanted to do something that involved animals.

She made an appointment to meet Dr. Louis Leakey, the famous scientist who studied the bones of dead animals. Curator of what is now the National Museum of Natural History in Kenya, he searched for clues about the origins and evolution of humans.

Dr. Leakey was the man who made Jane's dreams come true. When she met Dr. Leakey, he immediately offered her a job. His secretary had just quit, so he had an opening. Even if no position was available, he would have found something for Jane to do because he was so impressed by her deep interest in animals.

Before Jane began her secretarial work for Dr. Leakey, he invited her to assist him and his wife, Mary, on an expedition to Olduvai Gorge. The gorge lies in a remote spot in Tanganyika (now called Tanzania), the country south of Kenya. The Leakeys traveled to the gorge every summer to look for fossils, pieces of rock that contain evidence of life from ancient times. The Leakeys knew that apelike people had lived in the gorge millions of years ago. They already had found many tools that early humans had used, but they hoped to find skeletons, too.

Olduvai Gorge was remote and isolated. In those days, no roads went there. To get to the gorge, the Leakeys headed across the African plains in a jeep. Riding on the roof, Jane guided them by pointing out tracks left from the Leakeys' trip the year before. From her perch, she watched the show of a lifetime, all staged by nature itself. With no signs of human civilization in sight, Jane marveled at the rhinos, giraffes, and lions at home in the wild.

When the group arrived at the gorge, the digging began. Very carefully, the Leakeys and their assistants picked away at the ancient clay and rock. For hours they would find nothing. Then, with much excitement, someone would discover a bone or a fossil. Jane was awed by the prehistoric remains of life. When she found a bone, she tried to imagine what the animal it had come from might have been like—its size, color, smell, and character.

In the evenings, she and the other assistant, Gillian, roamed the gorge and the plains above it. They saw miniature antelopes, herds of gazelles and giraffes, and sometimes a black rhinoceros. Once when Jane and Gillian were walking through an area with bushes and low vegetation, they heard a growl. A young male lion stood only forty feet from them. They slowly backed away. The lion followed them, his tail twitching. Jane knew not to run. Like other cats, lions chase animals that run away. So Jane and Gillian walked slowly upward out of the gorge into an open area with no trees. The lion disappeared into the vegetation.

As the weeks at Olduvai passed, Dr. Leakey got to know Jane better. He told her about chimpanzees that lived in the rugged, tree-covered mountains near Lake Tanganyika. He knew that remains of prehistoric humans were often found by lake shores. He thought that chimp behavior in similar conditions might teach us something about the behavior of our human ancestors. Only one person had tried to study chimpanzees in the wild. Professor Henry W. Nissen had been able to spend only two and a half months in the field. In that short time, he had learned little. Dr. Leakey believed at least two years of study would be required to gain worthwhile information about the chimps.

Jane listened eagerly. Studying chimpanzees in the wild was exactly the kind of work she wanted to do. Like Tarzan, she wished to live among the animals in the forest. But Jane doubted she would be considered qualified to do such research. She had no university training and no formal education in the study of animal

37

Jane Goodall and anthropologist Dr. Louis Leakey stand in front of their office in Nairobi. Dr. Leakey believed Jane's patience and love of animals would make her a successful field researcher.

behavior. She tried not to let herself think too much about the project.

After three months at Olduvai Gorge, the expedition returned to Nairobi, where Jane began her secretarial work at the museum. From the other staff members, she soaked up all the information she could about African animals. She also began caring for animals in need. People brought her strays, orphans, and captured wild animals they had rescued from African markets.

Her first pet was a galago named Levi. Similar to small squirrels, galagos have very large ears and a long, monkeylike tail. Galagos are nicknamed "bush babies" because their loud wails sound like babies crying. Levi spent his days sleeping in a bowl on top of a cupboard in Dr. Leakey's office. When someone new walked into the office, Levi woke up immediately. Then, in a flying leap, he bounded to the shoulder of whoever had entered. One visitor was so startled that Jane was afraid he was going to have a heart attack. Dr. Leakey simply laughed, saying that in Africa people need to be prepared for anything.

Jane believed wild animals should not be kept captive. She often left the door open at night so Levi could come and go as he pleased. He never went farther than the other museum buildings. As Jane cared for more and more animals, she gave them many chances to go free. She often visited the Langata Forest, near where Louis and Mary Leakey lived. She took animals with her and left her car door wide open, hoping they would run off into the forest. But as soon as she started up the car to leave, the animals came running back. Jane sadly realized that they had forgotten their natural ways.

After working at the museum for nine months, Jane had saved enough money to bring her mother to Africa to visit her. From the moment her plane arrived, Vanne Goodall loved Kenya. She made many friends—animal and human—and she and Jane talked seriously about Jane's future. Jane explained that she liked working at the museum, but she still hoped to work with living animals in the wild. After Vanne returned to England, Jane finally told Dr. Leakey about her dream.

When he responded, Jane could not believe her ears. Dr. Leakey said he had been hoping that Jane wanted to study the wild chimps. He believed her lack of classroom education would allow her to take on the project with an open mind. She would not be influenced by academic theories and arguments about animal research. Also, he believed she sincerely wanted to learn about animals, and she had the patience needed for the job.

Jane's dream was close to coming true! First, however, Dr. Leakey had to convince organizations that gave money for animal research that a young English woman—a former waitress and secretary—could do what had never been done before: study and learn about wild chimpanzees living in a remote African forest.

CHAPTER 4
GETTING TO GOMBE

While Dr. Leakey looked for money to support the study of wild chimps, Jane returned to England. She worked at the London Zoo in its television film library, but she spent every moment she could watching the zoo's chimpanzees. She promised herself that someday she would help them have better lives. She read everything she could find about chimps, but the only information available described animals in captivity.

Based on Dr. Leakey's recommendation, the Wilkie

Foundation in Illinois volunteered to fund a chimp study for six months. The only restriction was made by government officials in Kigoma, the area of Tanganyika where Jane would be working. The officials refused to allow Jane to live in the forest alone. She had to have a European companion. Jane invited her mother, who accepted with great excitement.

Jane and Vanne flew to Nairobi eager to organize their gear and head for the Gombe (GOM-bee) Stream Reserve, the forest by Lake Tanganyika where several groups of chimps lived. But there were setbacks from the beginning. First, fishermen on the shores of Lake Tanganyika were disagreeing over fishing rights, and the local warden would not allow Jane and Vanne to enter the area until the situation was safe. That might take months. In the meantime, Dr. Leakey arranged for Jane to begin a short, trial study of vervets, a kind of monkey that lived on an island in Lake Victoria.

To get to the island, Jane and Vanne boarded a little boat captained by Hassan, an African familiar with the area. Every day on the island Jane watched the monkeys from dawn to dusk. In the evening, Hassan picked her up at the beach. She, Vanne, and Hassan slept on the boat anchored near shore.

Jane quickly learned how to take good field notes, what clothes to wear, and which movements scared the monkeys and which did not. She also learned that fierce wild animals were not the only danger in the forest. One day when she was making her way along a path made by hippos, she heard a noise. She stopped and realized that the noise was getting closer. Hippos are known to attack people when they are frightened, so Jane tried to hide in the bushes. But the source of the noise was more frightening than any hippo. It was a hunter searching for crocodiles. He wore nothing but a loincloth, and he carried a sharp spear in one hand. Hunting crocodiles was against the law. The poacher would not want to be discovered.

Jane knew the man would see her as he walked by, so she decided to make the first move. She stepped into full view and said "How are you?" in the native language. The man raised his spear and pointed it straight at her. Jane thought he was about to kill her. Then he lowered his spear and began yelling. Jane knew only a few of the words he used, but she understood what he meant. After he went away, Jane returned to the beach where Hassan picked her up.

She told Hassan what had happened, and he struck a deal with the crocodile poachers camped on the far side of the island. They promised to leave Jane alone if she did not go near their camp. She kept away from them.

After almost four weeks of studying the monkeys, Jane received the message that she and her mother could go to Gombe. She hated to leave the vervet research project unfinished. She had just begun to identify individual monkeys and understand some of their behavior. But she knew her main work was to learn about the chimps, and now the chance had come.

Or so she thought.

More problems developed. Jane and Vanne made an 800-mile, three-day trip by Land Rover from Nairobi to Kigoma, the city nearest the Gombe Stream Reserve. When Jane and Vanne arrived in Kigoma, they discovered that violence had broken out in the Belgian Congo (now known as Zaire), only twenty-five miles away. Kigoma was crowded with people seeking safety and shelter from the war. Local leaders told Jane that she could not go to Gombe until things settled down.

Jane and Vanne helped the refugees all they could. They crowded themselves and their belongings into one small hotel room to make more space for the homeless. Then Jane and Vanne left the hotel and camped. One evening they and a few other volunteers made two thousand Spam sandwiches for the refugees. Within a week, the refugees were transported by train to Tanganyika's capital, Dar es Salaam. Jane and Vanne waited another week in Kigoma. Finally the local officials said it was safe for them to go to Gombe, twelve miles away.

On July 16, 1960, Jane, Vanne, and Dominic, an African cook, landed on the shores of Lake Tanganyika at the Gombe Stream Chimpanzee Reserve. Years later Jane wrote, "It was a day I shall remember all my life." They unloaded their tents, food, cooking supplies, medicines, bedding, clothes, binoculars, notebooks, pens, and paper. Twenty-six-year-old Jane was so excited that as soon as they finished setting up camp, she began exploring the area. She climbed to the top of a high peak.

Jane climbs high in the trees with her binoculars to look for chimpanzees.

Sitting on a big flat rock warmed by the late afternoon sun, she looked out over the rugged mountains she would soon know well. That night she pulled her cot out of the tent and slept under the stars, already feeling at home under the African sky.

Every morning Jane set her alarm clock for 5:30 a.m., ate a banana or a couple slices of bread, and drank a cup of coffee. Then she set off to look for chimps. She hiked up and down the steep mountains and climbed high in the trees. The dense forest stayed deep in shadows from the vines and leafy growth one hundred feet overhead. Jane looked and looked, but found no chimps. Dr. Leakey was right to think that whoever undertook this study needed a great deal of patience. He chose the right person—Jane had known patience ever since she was a four-year-old waiting for the hen to lay an egg!

Then one day a series of "pant-hoots," the long-distance calls made by chimps, echoed through the forest. The hoots, interrupted by loud breathing sounds, came from a group of chimps climbing a msulula tree filled with ripe fruit. Jane kept her binoculars focused on the tree for two hours, fascinated by the chimps' quiet, peaceful feasting. If any chimp caught a glimpse of her, she knew it would flee instantly. So she stayed on the other side of the valley. She sat in a small clearing almost opposite the slope with the msulula tree. Although Jane was frustrated because the leafy branches blocked much of her view, for ten days she watched as much as she could.

Jane did not want to miss anything, so for three nights she even slept curled up in a blanket at her observation point. She learned many interesting things about chimp behavior. Chimps sleep high in the trees, often thirty or forty feet above the ground. At night, in only a few minutes, they make their sleeping nests. First they bend small branches and weave them together to make individual platforms. Then they cushion the platforms with small, leafy twigs. Sometimes a pile of leaves serves as a pillow. Young chimp babies share a nest with their mothers. The other chimps make their own nests. Usually Jane woke up before the chimps did. She liked to watch them awaken and greet each other in the earliest light of dawn.

Chimpanzees rest in a tree nest. Jane learned that until about age three, baby chimps share a sleeping nest with their mothers.

During these first days of intensive observation, Jane also learned that the chimps do not remain in permanent groups. They shift around, and occasionally two separate groups combine into one large one. Sometimes males stay together, but at other times they join groups with females and youngsters.

When the msulula tree no longer bore fruit, the chimps looked elsewhere for food. As long as Jane was far away from them, they went about their normal activities. From a great distance, watching with her binoculars, she learned that the ever-changing groups made up one large community of about fifty chimps. They roamed across five valleys. Already slim, Jane lost weight because of the dawn-to-dusk exercise. She did not eat lunch, so she survived on her light breakfast and an occasional cup of coffee from her Thermos during the day. She always wore drab khaki shorts and a shirt that blended in with the vegetation. Her blond hair was pulled back in a simple ponytail.

At dusk she made her way back to camp. She carried samples of the leaves, flowers, seeds, stems, bark, and fruits the chimps ate so the chimps' diet could be identified. She saved her field notes to recopy by lamp-light every night. Over a dinner of baked beans and corned beef, Jane and Vanne swapped stories about the day.

Jane described the chimps' activities as best she could. The chimps still ran off if she tried to study them closely, but at least she was getting a general picture of their lives. Jane also told Vanne about the other animals she encountered: baboons, monkeys, huge gray bush pigs, squirrels, snakes, enormous hairy spiders, giant centipedes, and mongooses, the small mammals known for killing deadly snakes.

Vanne described her days, too. She told about her repeated efforts to chase away baboons who stole the slightest bit of food left out on a table or cot. She described her disgust at waking up in the morning to find a deadly giant centipede clinging to the roof of the tent above her bed. And she told Jane about the medical treatments she gave at her clinic.

Under a simple thatched roof supported by four poles, Vanne handed out basic medical supplies like aspirin, iodine, and bandages to local fishermen and their families. One very sick man was helped there. Two huge sores had caused his leg to swell, and the infection had begun eating away at the bone. He refused to be treated at the Kigoma hospital, saying that people who went there died. Vanne helped him drip warm salt water over the sores, and in three weeks the swelling disappeared. Slowly his leg healed, and word about Vanne's doctoring spread. The clinic helped Jane and Vanne enjoy good relations with their human neighbors on the lake.

Then an illness struck that Vanne's medicines could not treat. Jane and Vanne both came down with malaria. The doctor in Kigoma had told them that there was no malaria in that region, so they had no drugs to fight it. For nearly two weeks they sweated with fever. With a temperature of one hundred and five degrees, Vanne became delirious and sometimes wandered from her tent. One morning Dominic found her lying unconscious by one of the palm trees. The malaria came close to killing both Jane and Vanne.

Most people would have given up after three months of frustrating, difficult research followed by a deadly illness. But Jane was no quitter. When she recovered, she was more determined than ever to succeed with her work. In fact, she worried that she might not be allowed to stay at Gombe much longer. If she did not uncover new information about the chimps, she thought that funding would stop and she would have to leave.

Vanne finally recovered from malaria, and after five months at Gombe, she needed to return to England. Before she left, she gave her daughter lots of encouragement. At first, Jane missed her terribly. But Jane said, "As the weeks passed, I accepted aloneness as a way of life and was no longer lonely. I was utterly absorbed in the work, fascinated by the chimps."

Jane's hard work soon paid off.

where Jane had been. He marked it with his droppings.

Jane spent so much time on the Peak that it began to feel like home. When the chimps slept near it, Jane did too. Jane knew that a leopard, buffalo, or poisonous snake could kill a human, and there were times she felt frightened. Only fools could be fearless in the forest. But Jane did not let fear stand in her way. She continued her work, climbing up and down the steep slopes and clawing her way through vines and bushes. With envy she watched chimps move easily through the vegetation and swing through the treetops high above the forest floor.

Over the months, Jane learned to recognize individual chimps, all of whom she named. Observing David Graybeard led her to two major discoveries— chimps use tools and eat meat. Excited by Jane's progress, research sponsors agreed to extend her study. This was just before the rainy day when the group of angry males had surrounded but not harmed her.

Only once did a chimp purposely hurt her. It happened on another rainy day when Jane held a thin piece of plastic over her for protection. She heard chimps nearby. She lay down flat, hoping they would not see her and run away. She stayed still, listening to footsteps coming very close. There was a flurry of activity in some nearby bushes, then a loud screech. A big male chimp came within only a few feet of Jane. He opened his mouth wide and angrily screamed at her. She saw his yellow teeth and pink tongue. Then he bolted behind her. Jane noticed a female and a young chimp watching silently from a tree. Then the big male's footsteps came near again, until he stood so close that she could hear his breathing. He let out a sudden bark and then hit Jane on the head. She sat up and looked into his eyes. He stared back at her and then walked off, frequently turning around to look at her again.

Years later, when Jane knew the individual chimps well, she concluded that the angry male must have been J.B., who often seemed fearless and irritable. She guessed that he was confused by her lying so still. Was she dead? When she sat up after he hit her, his question was answered. Also, he may have wondered about the strange plastic sheet over her. Perhaps he thought this shiny creature was another intruder in the forest, and he wanted to investigate.

As the weeks passed, the chimps gradually paid Jane less attention. Soon she would be accepted for what they may have believed her to be: a strange-looking, odd-smelling, skinny white ape.

Meanwhile, Dr. Leakey worried that Jane might not be accepted by the world's scientific community. He knew that scientists would question her research if she was not associated with a well-known university. Jane promised Dr. Leakey she would earn her Ph.D., the highest academic degree given by a university.

The first year Jane spent studying wild animals at Gombe was the education she had always dreamed of. She hated the idea of leaving Africa to sit in a college classroom. But in 1961 Jane began what she called her first of several "six-month exiles" at Cambridge University in England, far away from the chimps. Jane had no bachelor's degree, which students normally complete before beginning their Ph.D. studies. Cambridge University allowed Jane to skip the bachelor's and begin working on her Ph.D.

The scientists at the university—most of whom were

men—conducted research in terms of numbers and facts. Unlike Jane, they did not trust intuition and feelings. Jane's patient observation of the animals, and her emotional understanding of them, were very different from the usual scientific approach. At that time, few scientists believed animals had personalities. On one of her first papers, a professor changed all Jane's references to a chimp as "he" or "she" to "it." Jane changed them back. She could not imagine assigning numbers to David Graybeard or Goliath. The chimps were individuals—not "its"—with their own special personalities.

Dr. Leakey chose Jane to study the chimps because she loved animals and she had an open mind. Her patient way of getting to know the chimps gave her knowledge never gained before. Thanks to Jane's success, scientists all over the world eventually changed their attitudes about studying animals. But at first, just as Dr. Leakey had warned Jane, many scientists did not approve of her.

Jane was much happier learning to fit in with the chimps at Gombe than she was trying to fit in with the professors at the university. After her first six months at Cambridge, Jane had only one desire—to return to

Africa. Her worst fear was that the chimps would forget her and run away when they saw her.

They remembered her well.

David Graybeard still visited her camp, often with a companion or two. One morning David calmly helped himself to a handful of bananas from the table in front of Jane's tent. He took them to the edge of camp and began munching. Goliath, sitting nearby, did not dare come as close to Jane's tent as David had. Having no bananas himself, he greedily watched David enjoy his feast. Slowly Goliath put his hand to David's face. David gently spit out the banana in his mouth and handed it to Goliath, who chewed it some more before swallowing.

Goliath was the most powerful male. In chimp society, each male competes for a high rank. To become number one, a male rarely hurts other chimps seriously. Instead, he shows off his strength in what Jane calls "displays." A male might run through the forest hurling rocks and branches. He tries to look as big and fierce as he can. Sometimes males charge, but they usually swerve at the last minute to avoid a real fight. The top male might stay in power for

A curious chimp watches Jane enjoy a cup of coffee in her tent. The Gombe chimps grew used to Jane's presence and frequently came into camp.

Photo by Baron Hugo van Lawick. Courtesy of National Geographic Society.

several years, but ranks are constantly tested.

When Goliath was number one, the other chimps stayed out of his way. They gave him the best spots for building sleeping nests, and he led during any conflicts with baboons or other competitors for food. Goliath was the chimp who shook branches above Jane during the first threatening encounter with the male chimps in which she was surrounded.

William, another male who often accompanied David Graybeard, was very different from Goliath. He acted passive and timid. If Jane moved quickly, or if baboons made a noisy rush for the supply of bananas, William backed off. He would make a chimp's face of submission by pulling his lips into a sickly looking smile.

All the chimps spent hours every day grooming each other. They picked off flakes of dry skin, or small twigs tangled in their hair. The touching seemed to comfort them in the same way that people relax with a back scratch or a gentle pat on the shoulder. Sometimes one chimp draped an arm around another's shoulders, or they held hands.

David was the first chimp to fully accept Jane. She

followed him so much that she began to believe he waited for her, just as he might wait for Goliath or William. Chimps moved through the trees and the undergrowth much more quickly than she could. Often when she trailed behind David, she doubted she would ever catch up with him. But then she would spot him sitting and looking in her direction. As soon as he saw her, he would turn and continue on his way.

Jane grew to appreciate the chimps' intelligence more and more. She observed them making tools in addition to the termite fishing poles. They made sponges by pulling a handful of leaves off a branch. After chewing on the leaves, the chimps poked them into places where water had collected, such as the hollow in a fallen tree. The chimps then sucked on the leaf sponges, getting the most water from them they could.

Jane shared her findings with Dr. Leakey. Convinced that Jane's work should be captured in a documentary film, he sent a twenty-five-year-old National Geographic Society photographer named Hugo van Lawick to Gombe. Hugo was a Dutch baron, meaning his family belonged to the nobility in the Netherlands. Hugo had come to Africa to photograph animals that he loved. Dr. Leakey wanted Jane and Hugo to meet. He predicted that they would make a perfect match for each other. But he felt it would not be appropriate for them to be alone at camp. He persuaded the National Geographic Society to pay for Vanne to visit Gombe at the same time Hugo was there.

Jane doubted the chimps would accept Hugo, a second strange white ape in the forest, especially since he carried a lot of whirring, shiny camera equipment. Yet the chimps quickly accepted him. In fact, they began coming to the camp more often. They discovered treats in addition to the bananas. For them, chewing cardboard was a delight, as was sucking on sweaty clothes and well-used blankets! One time Hugo wrapped an old shirt around his camera to cover its shiny surface. He was startled when the camera jerked in his hands for no apparent reason. David Graybeard had grabbed the shirt and nearly pulled the camera away with it!

A few days before Hugo left Gombe in November 1962, he took pictures of David, William, and Goliath termite fishing. For the first time, chimps were photographed making and using tools. Hugo had taken the best photographs and films of wild chimps ever made. The *National Geographic* magazine containing his pictures and an article about Jane's work was so popular that it sold out.

Jane missed Hugo a great deal after he left Gombe. To cheer herself up, she decorated her own Christmas tree with silver paper and cotton. The "presents" underneath it were an unusually generous pile of bananas. On December 25, Goliath and William visited Jane at camp. Thrilled by the treats awaiting them, the two chimps jumped up and down, threw their arms around each other, and screamed in excitement. Then they feasted.

Later in the day, something very special happened. David Graybeard paid Jane a visit. Calm as usual, he sat close to her while he helped himself to bananas. Slowly Jane reached over to touch him, using the grooming movements she had seen the chimps use. At first David brushed her hand gently away. He did not seem alarmed, so Jane tried again. She parted the hair on his back, scratching lightly at flecks of dirt and flakes of dry skin. She groomed him for at least a minute before he

Photo by Baron Hugo van Lawick. Courtesy of National Geographic Society.

Jane gently grooms David Graybeard while he munches bananas. David Graybeard was the first chimp to allow Jane's touch.

pushed her hand gently away again.

Jane had touched a wild chimp! David had given her a Christmas gift she would never forget.

Another unforgettable gift was free admission to a rain dance. One day a loud clap of thunder announced the beginning of a downpour, and a male chimp at the top of a ridge began stamping his feet and making louder and louder pant-hoots. Jane gasped as he charged full speed down the steep hillside. About thirty yards from the ridge top, he grabbed a small tree, swung around its trunk, and leaped onto a low branch. He looked up the slope and watched two more males charge after him. They grabbed branches and waved them as they ran. It seemed to Jane that they had taken on nature itself, showing off their own strength in the face of the storm. Then all the males slowly climbed back up to the ridge top to repeat the high-energy display again and again. Not far from Jane, females and youngsters watched the spectacular twenty-minute performance.

Jane grew more and more attached not only to the chimps, but also to their environment. She wrote, "I loved to sit in a forest when it was raining, and to hear the pattering of the drops on the leaves and feel utterly enclosed in a dim twilight world of greens and browns and dampness." After a day of rain or a night of heavy dew, the vegetation remained drenched, making it impossible for anyone in the forest to stay dry. The chimps often shivered and caught colds and coughs. Jane's wet clothes chilled her, so she decided not to wear them. After leaving her warm tent in the pre-dawn darkness, she tucked her clothes into a plastic bag to keep them dry. She then scrambled up the muddy mountainside. Wet grasses, sometimes as high as twelve feet, tickled and scratched her skin until it toughened up. Once she got to the Peak, she put her dry clothes on. She was glad to get warm, but she felt guilty that the chimps could not share that luxury.

Jane loved her special relationship with David Graybeard. "One day," she said, "as I sat near him at the bank of a tiny trickle of crystal-clear water, I saw a ripe red palm nut lying on the ground. I picked it up and held it out to him on my open palm. He turned his head away. When I moved my hand closer he looked at it, and then at me, and then he took the fruit, and at the same time

71

held my hand firmly and gently with his own." At that moment, Jane believed the soft pressure of David's fingers spoke to her on an emotional level that crossed the barrier between humans and chimpanzees. She said, "It was a reward far beyond my greatest hopes."

Much less rewarding to Jane was her yearly trip to Cambridge University to work on her Ph.D. She hated to leave Gombe. But during her third year's stay in England, she had reason to celebrate. She became a bride.

During Hugo's repeated visits to Gombe, he and Jane fell in love. In 1964 they got married in London. They included as much of Gombe in the event as possible. A statue of David Graybeard adorned the wedding cake, and large portraits of David, Goliath, and other chimps decorated the reception hall.

Jane and Hugo cut their honeymoon short not because something was wrong, but because something exciting had happened.

Flo, one of the first chimps Jane had known at Gombe, had given birth. Jane and Hugo couldn't wait to see the new baby.

CHAPTER 6
BABIES AND BANANAS

Flo's bright-eyed infant Flint looked every bit as cuddly as Jubilee, Jane's lovable toy chimp. His little wrinkled face and sleek black hair contrasted with his smooth, hairless pink tummy and hands. His ears were round, pink, and perfectly shaped in comparison with his old mother's torn and ragged ones.

Within a few days of the birth of any new baby chimp, excited chimps gather around to get a good look. A nervous mother may try to brush the onlookers away before their curiosity has been satisfied. Then the frustrated chimps are likely to leap into the trees, vigorously sway the branches, and jump around dangerously close to the mother and baby.

Old Flo knew better than to interfere with the chimps' examination of the baby. An experienced mother, she already had three youngsters: Faben (eleven years old), Figan (eight), and Fifi (five). She patiently allowed everyone to take a good look at her newest son when he was only a few days old.

But looking at him and touching him were two different things. For the first three months, Flo, like most chimp mothers, allowed no one else to handle her baby. (The father is unknown because females mate with many different males.) Fascinated by her baby brother, Flo's daughter Fifi kept trying to touch him. Flo pushed her hand away every time. Fifi learned how to sneak a few touches. She would groom her mother, slowly moving her fingers closer and closer to the baby. Then she briefly handled Flint's tiny fingers, glancing nervously at her mother. Quickly she began grooming Flo again as if she had done nothing out of the ordinary.

Photo by Baron Hugo van Lawick/National Geographic Image Collection.

A baby chimp lies content in his mother's arms and sucks his thumb. Jane learned that baby chimps are like human babies in several stages of development.

When Flint was about three months old, he began showing interest in his sister. She responded with an eager caress. But if Fifi ever seemed the slightest bit rough, Flo instantly pushed Fifi away and cuddled the baby, kissing him and allowing him to nurse until he felt secure. As Flint grew, Flo gradually allowed Fifi to handle him more, but always under her watchful eye.

By the time Flint was five months old, he was strong enough to cling by himself to Flo's belly as she traveled around the forest. On many days she wandered for several miles, eating berries and leaves, drinking at the stream, and greeting other chimps. Soon she began pushing Flint up on her back, where he learned to ride jockey-style. Flo could move much more easily without a baby hanging below her, and Flint could enjoy a right-side-up view of the world. Fifi learned from her mother's example and let Flint ride on her back, too.

Flint tried taking his first steps at about five months old, wobbling like a human toddler. He also tried to climb trees. Time and time again, he tumbled backwards, a muddle of mixed-up hands, feet, and leaves. Flo's protective hands were always there to catch him.

Besides protecting Flint, Flo also played with him. Sometimes she lay on her back and supported him with one foot. Flint laughed as she tickled him and jostled him up and down. She rolled around on the ground and even tried a somersault, joining Flint and her other youngsters in a family free-for-all. But even Figan, at eight a teenager by chimpanzee standards, never dared play too roughly around the baby. He did not want to face his mother's disapproval.

One time when Fifi was holding Flint, Flint looked up at Figan and held out his arms as if wanting to be picked up. Figan acted confused, but Flint leaned closer and nuzzled Figan's chest, perhaps thinking he could nurse. When Flint uttered a small cry of frustration, Flo hurried over. Seeing his mother approach, a concerned-looking Figan held up both his hands in a gesture that seemed to say "Not guilty."

As Flint's physical abilities increased, so did his curiosity. If an object or animal interested him, he leaned toward it, set his arms and legs in motion, and pushed off in the direction he wanted to go. He expected attention from everyone, and he usually got it. Adult males seemed

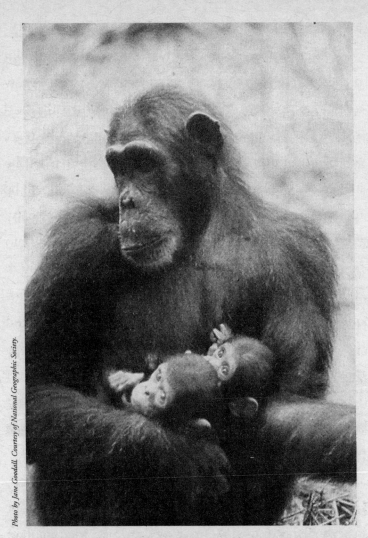

A chimp mother holds her twin babies. Mothers kiss and cuddle their babies like human mothers do. Females learn nurturing skills by observing and helping mother chimps care for their young.

to pat him just so he would then leave them alone.

One afternoon when Flo was termite fishing, Flint played nearby. Figan had eaten his fill, and he grew restless. Impatient to leave, he started down the trail toward the stream. Flo gave no sign of being ready to go. Several more times, Figan walked away, but when he looked back and saw that his mother had not budged, he returned. Then he got an idea. He whimpered at baby Flint, who innocently allowed himself to be lifted onto his big brother's back. With Flint riding high, Figan walked down the trail. Flo hurried after. Faben and Fifi observed their brother's trick, and later they imitated him. They "kidnapped" little Flint to get their mother to move along when they were bored.

Hugo photographed Flint's early childhood and helped with much of the work at Gombe. He and Jane put their heads together to solve a growing problem.

The number of people living at camp had increased. Hassan, the captain of the boat Jane and Vanne had slept in when Jane studied the monkeys at Lake Victoria, had joined the crew. In addition, a scientist had come to study the plants of the area. Living with the cook Dominic were his wife and daughter. The growing human population was not in itself a problem. The trouble was the growing popularity of the humans' camp with the animals.

Chimps and baboons loved to eat the bananas and chew the clothing. Nowhere near as timid as the chimps, baboons swarmed around the camp, stealing food at every opportunity. The greed of some of the top-ranking male chimps was also a problem. A single chimp might devour fifty bananas in one sitting while younger males got none. Several chimps had seen David Graybeard enter a tent and select bedding and shirts to suck on, and they began doing the same. Some chimps had even invaded the huts of local families. Someone could be hurt, for few people realized how much the chimps had lost their fear of humans. The situation had to be corrected, but how?

Jane did not want to stop feeding the chimps bananas, because when the chimps were close, Hugo could snap excellent photos, and Jane could easily make detailed observations. The solution was to move the bananas away from the humans' tents at the beach.

Hassan built cement boxes in one of the valleys about a half mile from the lake. The boxes were put in the ground. Controls connected by long wires many yards away allowed people to open them. To lead the chimps to the new feeding station, Jane and Hugo moved their tents near it. Jane planned to wait there until chimps happened to pass by. Then she would offer them a banana.

The first morning after the move, Hugo stayed at the beach, communicating with Jane by walkie-talkie. He reported that a group of chimps had arrived, and he planned to try to lead them to the new banana give-away site. Jane heard little from Hugo until a breathless, crackling request came through on her walkie-talkie. Hugo asked her to drop bananas as fast as she could along the path leading from the new feeding station to the beach.

Hugo showed a banana to David Graybeard. Then Hugo picked up an empty box like the ones the bananas were usually stored in. He carried the box up the path toward the new feeding station. The plan worked better than Hugo had expected. David and his friends followed him excitedly. Hugo feared that the group might catch up with him, grab the box, and get very angry to find that it was empty. However, before that happened, the chimps came across the bananas Jane had dropped along the path. The chimps quickly learned to come to the new camp for their banana feed.

At the feeding station, Jane and Hugo hid in their tent, pulled the handle to open a banana box, and watched. They gained new appreciation for Figan's intelligence. As a young male, he had little chance to get many bananas when older males were around. But he found a way around this problem.

It is common for groups of chimps to wander from place to place, following no particular route or schedule. When any individual chimp rises and moves on, the others generally do too. On more than one occasion, Jane watched Figan casually walk away from the new feeding station. The other chimps slowly followed him. Ten minutes later, Figan returned by himself. Alone, he ate all the bananas he wanted. One time he returned to find high-ranking males there as well. In a tantrum of frustration, he screamed and hit the ground. Years later, as a mature chimp, he used his intelligence to become the number one male himself.

With the success of the new feeding station and the chimps' growing acceptance of humans, Jane realized that additional researchers could help record more information than she and Hugo could manage, even though they worked seven days a week and late into the night. She accepted requests of students begging for the chance to come to Gombe. Jane described the schedule that she, Hugo, and a new research assistant, Edna Koning, followed. "We worked all day and far into the night. I dictated my observations onto tape, which meant that I didn't have to take my eyes off the activity around me. Edna typed out the tapes in the evening while I struggled with analysis for my Ph.D. thesis. We started making an extra copy of my notes, three copies in all, and I marked this copy into categories of behavior— grooming, submission, aggression, and so forth. Edna, Hugo, and I cut these up and pasted them in their relevant sections into large notebooks. This of course was immensely helpful for my analysis. The third copy was always sent off every month to Louis for safekeeping in case of fire, flood, or some other catastrophe at the Gombe."

As the research center grew, so did Jane's fame. She was the first person to succeed in the study of wild chimps, and she paved the way for other women who shared Jane's love of apes and wanted to study them. Dr. Leakey helped two other famous scientists get started. One was Dian Fossey, who lived among the gorillas in central Africa. The other was Biruté Galdikas, who studied orangutans in Borneo. Today, half the researchers studying wild apes are women.

Directing the growing research center at Gombe became a big job for Jane. More tents were set up. The bolder chimps began rummaging through them, looking for clothes to chew on or a stash of bananas people had hoped to save for themselves. Hiding places had to be changed constantly. Clothes were locked up in tin trunks, but even that did not solve the problem.

One morning when Vanne was visiting Gombe, Jane heard a scream coming from her mother's tent. She ran over to investigate. David Graybeard was chewing on the pant leg of Vanne's pajamas, which she had half on and half off! As soon as Jane stopped laughing, she bribed David with a banana to let go of the pajamas.

When the clothes were locked up, the chimps started chewing on the canvas chairs, shoes, and even the tents. One time Jane returned from a day in the forest to find three chimps sitting next to a few scraps of canvas where her tent used to be. They had gnawed to shreds all but the metal frame of her tent!

Some clever male chimps decided not to eat the tents, but to use them in their displays of power. During their charges to impress other males, they pulled out the tent pegs one by one as they raced past. What a dramatic show the collapsing canvas made! It did not bother the chimps that the humans had to sort out the mess afterward.

And the mess was going to get worse.

CHAPTER 7

CHANGES

When Jane returned to Gombe in 1966 from finishing her Ph.D. at Cambridge, she found out that the chimps had begun hanging around the tents for hours every day. They were fighting more than she had ever seen before. The human intruders at Gombe had affected the chimps' behavior, a situation that Jane was determined to change.

Jane had been thrilled by Flo's allowing her to tickle and play with baby Flint. Now, however, she realized that as Flint grew older, his strength and his lack of fear of humans could make him very dangerous. Jane made a new rule. Humans were not allowed to touch the chimps.

The tents were replaced by aluminum buildings built further up the valley. Covered with grass, the buildings blended in well with the surroundings, and the chimps could be locked out.

Fights over the bananas at the feeding station had become frequent and dangerous among both the chimps and the baboons. Some chimps were more clever than the humans had expected. For example, Fifi, Figan, and their friend Evered had figured out how to open the banana boxes. A low-ranking male, Evered would open many boxes but then be pushed out of the way while more powerful chimps and baboons fought over the feast and grabbed all the goods.

Fifi and Figan were smarter. With Flo, they sat back and watched the males fight for the bananas. The winners would then stuff themselves. After the males wandered off, Fifi and Figan opened boxes and enjoyed the fruit with no competitors to bother them. In fact, Flo's family was becoming increasingly dependent on the humans. Jane did not want the animals to change their natural ways. So a new feeding system was built with an underground tunnel-like bunker. The staff could fill and control the opening of the boxes out of the animals' sight.

If baboons were around, the boxes were kept shut. If chimps happened to visit and no bananas were available, they wandered off. They quickly adjusted to the on-again, off-again banana supply, for they were used to trees that gave fruit for a few weeks but then were bare for months. The feeding station was maintained because the chimps stayed close by when the banana boxes were open. Researchers could easily observe them and keep track of ongoing changes in their relationships. One change was the position of number one male.

Usually a male's charging display is an act designed to make him look larger and stronger than he really is. Screaming, throwing branches, and bristling the hair on their backs, charging males try to frighten other males in order to rise in the ladder of power. They rarely fight, but they often test their rank by using scare tactics. Goliath's reign as number one male ended when Mike came up with a brilliant show unmatched by any of the other chimps.

Mike learned how to make a huge racket using empty kerosene cans left around the camp. When he staged a display, he kicked cans, banged them together, or threw them in the air. Terrified chimps and humans scattered when Mike charged. Once Jane did not get out of the way fast enough, and she got hit in the head by a flying can.

Mike's number one position was pretty well established by the time the kerosene cans were locked away. But Goliath continued to test Mike. One time Jane watched Mike and Goliath take turns putting on spectacular shows of their strength. In a tree they swayed, shook branches, screamed, and flexed their muscles. Then they ran through the undergrowth, throwing rocks and anything else in their path. Mike and Goliath charged at each other, but they never attacked. After their half-hour duel, peace was restored. The two chimps sat down like best friends and calmly groomed each other for an hour.

There were many friendships in the chimp

Young chimp playmates often show affection for each other by hugging, wrestling, tickling each other, and swinging together on tree limbs.

community. Flint loved to play with Melissa's son Goblin. They would swing on vines, chase each other around a tree trunk, or romp and wrestle with one another. If either one of them happened to bump into an adult male, they would usually receive a gentle pat. If they tried to climb a tree, any nearby adult might help boost them up to a branch. But if a new group of chimps arrived on the scene, tensions instantly soared. Mothers rushed to grab their little ones, for they knew Mike and perhaps some of the other males would stage violent charging displays for the newcomers. Once the authority of the dominant males was confirmed, the submissive chimps would be reassured by a gentle touch of the powerful males. Calm would return to the community. One mother, however, seemed not to worry much about her offspring even when danger was near. This chimp mother was named Passion.

The opposite of Flo, Passion almost ignored her young daughter Pom. She did not hold her while she nursed, so Pom rarely got enough milk. In downpours, Pom tried to ride under Passion's belly to be protected from the rain, but Passion pushed her onto her back,

Most chimp mothers allow their babies to ride on their backs for security—and to get a better look at the world.

which made it easier to move through the underbrush. Pom never dared stray far from Passion. When Passion was ready to go, she could not be counted on to wait for Pom. Pom had to scramble as fast as her unsteady little legs would carry her to catch up when her mother headed away.

Baby chimps rely on their mothers for at least four years, and family loyalty appears to be lifelong. Passion's lack of concern for her baby showed her to be strangely different from all the other chimp mothers. In the years to come, the entire chimp community would feel the effects of her abnormal behavior.

At the moment, the community was feeling the terrible effects of an epidemic. Chimps are so similar to humans that they can catch many human diseases. At first, Jane was puzzled when an infant chimp died. She then discovered that polio, a crippling and often fatal disease, had broken out among people living in an area south of Gombe where chimps were known to roam. The polio virus can spread quickly.

Jane radioed to Dr. Leakey to have polio vaccine flown to Gombe for the staff, the local people, and the chimps. Jane kept careful records to try to be sure each chimp got the right amount of vaccine, which was hidden in bananas. For some, the vaccine came too late. J.B., the cranky old male, disappeared and was assumed to have died of the disease. Faben, Flo's oldest son, lost the use of one arm. Melissa's neck and shoulders were affected.

Jane cried to see the slow, painful course of the disease in one of the chimps she had known since she first came to Gombe. When Jane had been a newcomer in the forest and he shook branches at her, she was reminded of Peter Rabbit being chased from the garden in Beatrix Potter's famous tales. She named the chimp Mr. McGregor. He was easy to recognize because his head was almost bald except for a thin halo of hair. Jane believed that the chimp named Humphrey might be McGregor's younger brother, for they spent a lot of time together. When McGregor's legs became paralyzed from polio, all the chimps but Humphrey kept away from him. The chimps hugged each other for comfort when they saw McGregor. Only Humphrey stayed near him.

His condition got worse. Within days, he could barely pull himself along using his arms, and his legs were useless. He tried desperately to stay with the other chimps. One afternoon he painfully somersaulted in order to move forward. Slowly, and after resting many times, he managed to get close to a group of grooming males in a tree. With great effort he pulled himself into the tree and reached up to greet them. Jane cried in sympathy when she saw the chimps move away from him. Exhausted, Mr. McGregor simply sat and stared.

Flies swarmed around sores that had developed all over his body. He allowed Jane to spray them. She brought him food on a plate of leaves that she lifted up to a nest he had made before. Unlike healthy chimps who make a new nest every night, he used the same one over and over.

Goliath attacked McGregor, who could do nothing but curl into a ball while Goliath pounded on him. When a second male seemed about to do the same, Jane and Hugo bravely stood in front of McGregor, and the male chimp swerved the other way. Only Humphrey remained loyal, although even he did not touch the sickly, dying chimp. Once, however, he dared to scare off the more powerful Goliath, who was displaying near McGregor.

When Mr. McGregor dislocated an arm, Jane knew the end was near. He was very weak and had only one usable arm. He could not survive much longer. On his last night, Jane saw him look longingly up into a tree. He could neither climb to a nest nor make one. Jane made a pile of vegetation that he somehow managed to roll onto. The next morning while Jane gave old Mr. McGregor his favorite breakfast—two eggs—Hugo used a pistol to end the chimp's misery.

That was one of the hardest jobs Jane and Hugo shared. Most of the time they enjoyed their work together. Because National Geographic could not afford to keep a photographer full-time at Gombe, Jane sometimes went with Hugo to locations where he photographed animals other than chimpanzees.

One time they traveled to Ngorongoro Crater, a valley left when the volcano "blew its top" thousands of years ago. Jane loved the beautiful grassland, trees, lake, and small rivers. While Hugo took photos, she studied the hyenas who lived in the area. Together they wrote a book on hyenas, jackals, and wild dogs, called *Innocent Killers*.

In camp late one evening, Jane and Hugo heard screams coming from the kitchen tent and the sound of ripping canvas. Hugo peeked outside their tent. Between them and the Land Rover—the safest place in camp—stood a lion!

Jane lit their small gas stove so that if the lion tore their tent open, they could set newspaper on fire. Then they could try to scare the lion away by waving the burning paper in his face. Hugo looked outside the tent again and saw that the lion had moved, so he jumped into the car. He inched it forward and Jane jumped in, too. Shining the headlights, they saw three young male lions, which they herded away from camp. Then they realized they had left the stove burning. A loose tent flap had caught fire. They put the blaze out with a fire extinguisher and were finally sitting down to dinner when they heard a warning yell from the cook's tent. The lions had returned.

The curious animals ripped more canvas and pushed their heads into the tents. Jane and Hugo gave up on the idea of trying to stay in their burned tent and drove to an empty log cabin nearby. When they got there, they discovered a very large lion on the front step! And on the back step a lioness was eating a recently killed antelope. Jane and Hugo waited until the lion in front left. Busy with her feast, the lioness in back did not notice them hurry into the cabin, which they locked up tight.

Jane and Hugo later returned to Ngorongoro. This time they brought their baby with them. Hugo Eric Louis van Lawick was born in 1967. Some Africans who knew about Jane and Hugo's close call with the lions in camp suggested their baby be called Simba, the Swahili word for lion. But for some reason that Jane can't remember, Grub was the nickname that stuck.

Figuring out how to raise Grub safely when they went back to Gombe was the biggest challenge Jane had ever faced. But she was determined to find a way.

CHAPTER 8

PARADISE IN DANGER

Chimps sometimes eat baby baboons, and Jane knew that years earlier some chimps had stolen two African babies for food. How could Jane protect Grub once she was back at Gombe?

She put him in a cage! It was a good-sized playpen enclosed all around. Sometimes Humphrey, Evered, and other males peered in, rattling the bars threateningly. When he felt mischievous, Grub teased the baboons, who were even more numerous than the chimps. He had fun raising his eyebrows and staring at them. Feeling threatened, the baboons banged on his cage, but Grub was safe behind its bars. When Grub began walking, Jane built a house near the beach where the chimps and baboons rarely roamed. The house had a large enclosed porch where Grub could play safely.

Jane modeled her parenting on what she considered to be two excellent examples: her own mother, Vanne, and Flo, the most successful chimp mother at Gombe. Jane spent less time with the chimps and played with Grub for hours when he was young. As much as possible, Jane and Hugo took Grub with them wherever they went. When he was old enough to attend school, Jane did not send him away. Instead, she hired tutors to come to Gombe.

Grub's unusual childhood taught him much that English or American children would never experience. For example, he knew to kick the walls of the outhouse before entering. This was not a knock to ask if someone was already using the outhouse. Rather, it was a good hard kick intended to dislodge poisonous centipedes, bats, and wolf spiders. Grub survived ten bouts with malaria. As a two-year-old he was attacked by angry safari ants, whose bites could have killed him if Hugo had not managed to brush them off in time.

Hugo also saved Grub from a baboon attack. Like chimps, baboons have long memories. One male baboon seemed to remember Grub teasing him from the safety of the cage. Once Grub climbed a tree for fun, and the baboon jumped toward him, his large fangs bared. Grub screamed, and Hugo pulled him from the tree just before the baboon's jaws closed on him.

But Hugo was not always at Gombe. He traveled a great deal in order to work on photography assignments. Jane left Gombe as seldom as possible. They spent less and less time together. In 1974, when Grub was seven years old, Jane and Hugo separated and divorced.

The chimps were splitting up, too. Several individuals, including Goliath, moved to the southern part of the range, separating themselves from the main chimp group. Previously, chimp "patrols" from the Gombe community had fought with chimps whose ranges bordered on their own. Fights between males *within* the community rarely lasted a whole minute, with the

Ready for a fight! Groups of angry male chimps may attack other chimps in brutal, humanlike warfare.

shrieks and commotion being far greater than any actual harm to the chimps involved. However, attacks against outsiders were serious. Now the southern group became a new community, and the northerners, led by Mike and the increasingly strong Figan, would not allow the southerners near them.

For four years, when males from the northern and southern communities met, they displayed, charged, and violently attacked each other. Before a battle, the males would often huddle, grinning with excitement and fear. Then, as a cooperative group, they attacked individuals or small groups of chimps. The northerners outnumbered the southerners, and one by one they killed the rebels. Jane was horrified when Figan killed her old friend Goliath. As a youngster, Figan had imitated him when Goliath was the number one male. Jane recognized that chimps were similar to humans in yet another way— they took part in organized, aggressive war.

Then in 1975 a human attack occurred. Forty armed men from Zaire crossed the lake during the night and kidnapped four students from Gombe. They were tied up and taken to Zaire. Jane and the other Europeans and

Americans left the camp. Only the African field staff remained. Everyone prayed that the kidnap victims were alive and would be returned. After weeks of worry, Jane was filled with relief when the last of the victims was released unharmed.

Within the chimp community, kidnapping victims did not have the same good fortune. Gilka's first baby, a healthy male named Gandalf, disappeared when he was about a month old. At first, no one could imagine what had happened to him. The most likely—and horrifying— explanation came later. Gilka had a second baby, named Otta. One afternoon Gilka calmly sat holding her infant. Passion, who had ignored and sometimes treated her own daughter Pom very roughly, stared at the newborn. Then she charged toward them. Gilka fled, screaming. It was a struggle for her to run and support her baby. Her left arm, wrist, and hand had been paralyzed by polio, and she was no match for Passion. Passion grabbed the infant and killed it instantly with a deep bite on the head. Passion, Pom, and her younger brother Prof ate the baby.

The next year Gilka gave birth to another son, Orion. For protection, she stayed in the company of males, and she was terrified whenever Passion came near. The males attacked Passion and chased her off. However, one warm day Gilka sat alone with Orion resting in the shade. Pom quietly approached through the underbrush, followed by her mother. Pom and Passion attacked, seriously wounding Gilka. They stole the baby and ate it. The pair probably killed at least eight other chimp infants as well. Passion and Pom finally stopped killing infants when they became pregnant themselves.

Flo's daughter Fifi was the only female from the main chimp community whose infant during that time was not killed by Passion and Pom. But death had taken old Flo. She had crossed from the living to the dead at the same time she was crossing a stream. When Jane heard the news, she rushed to the stream. There lay her old friend, one of the first chimps she had known at Gombe. Jane spent the night nearby, protecting the body from bush pigs.

Also nearby was Flo's eight-year-old son, Flint. When Flo had tried to stop nursing him at age four, he put on such wild temper tantrums that Flo often gave in to him. After she had another baby, Flint grew terribly jealous. That baby disappeared (Jane did not know what happened to her), and Flint seemed to try to replace her, acting almost like an infant himself. Now that his mother was dead, he was filled with grief.

Flint might have turned to his older sister Fifi for comfort, but at the time of Flo's death, she had roamed out of the area for a few days. Although Flint spent time with his older brother Figan, he never overcame his depression. He acted lazy and lost his interest in food. When Fifi returned, she groomed him and encouraged him to travel with her. He did not. Even though he was physically able to take care of himself, he seemed emotionally unable to go on without his mother. He curled up on the ground very near the place in the stream where Flo's dead body had lain three weeks before. He stared at the water waiting until death took him from the world he no longer cared to live in.

Although 1975 held many tragedies for Gombe, the year brought good news, too. Jane married Derek Bryceson, an Englishman. Director of Tanzania's wildlife parks, he was devoted to animals. Like Jane, he had spirit and determination that allowed him to persevere when most other people would have quit.

When Derek was a nineteen-year-old fighter pilot during World War II, his plane had been shot down. He injured his spine, and doctors said he would never walk again. They were wrong. Derek managed to teach himself to walk by leaning on a stick. After earning a degree at Cambridge in agriculture, he turned down a job in England, which he said was nothing more than "armchair farming, suitable for an invalid." He moved to Africa, ran a successful wheat farm, and eventually settled in Tanzania's capital, Dar es Salaam. Active in politics, he served as a member of Parliament, minister of agriculture, and minister of health.

After the kidnapping of the foreign students, Jane decided that the researchers at Gombe must be mainly local people. Well-known and popular, Derek gave great encouragement to the African staff. The Africans stopped seeing themselves as helpers needing "Dr. Jane" for leadership. They gained confidence and interest in their work, becoming top-notch independent researchers.

The chimp community continued to change. Making the most of his strength and intelligence, Flo's son Figan became the number one male. Figan allowed Goblin, the former playmate of his little brother Flint, to tag around after him. Figan was clearly Goblin's hero. As an adolescent, Goblin imitated Figan's displays and studied his techniques for keeping his high rank.

Goblin was an excellent student. Just as he had observed Figan taking advantage of another male's weakness, Goblin chose his moments carefully to try to topple Figan. One time when Figan had hurt the fingers of his right hand, Goblin dared to display before him. He had learned from Figan the value of a surprise display by startling sleeping males or leaping up from a hidden spot in the undergrowth to unnerve a relaxed chimp.

Goblin even challenged Jane and some of the other humans. Jane called him a pest for grabbing her wrists. If she tried to shake him off, he gripped tighter. Rather than feeling afraid, Jane considered his behavior irritating because she could not take notes while he held her arms. So when she saw him coming toward her, she smeared her wrists and hands with oil, margarine, or any other slippery substance. Goblin did not like to get his hands greasy, so he learned to leave her hands alone.

He probably considered Jane to be another female who must be dominated if he were to succeed in becoming the number one male. So he found another way to pester her. For several years, Jane never knew when he might charge out of the undergrowth, run up behind her, and give her a slap or even stamp on her back. Because she never fought back, he finally stopped hassling her. He probably believed his rank had been confirmed.

Goblin continued to challenge Figan, who ultimately disappeared. Jane did not know if he became ill and died, or if he was killed by neighboring chimps. But after Figan was gone, Goblin used the skills he had learned during Figan's ten-year reign to take over the leadership position himself. He had no way of knowing at the time that Figan's nephew, Freud, would become top male in his turn, too. Among the chimps, just as among humans, life and change go hand in hand.

CHAPTER 9
FOR ALL OF US

As Jane's reputation grew, more and more people wanted to meet and hear the famous expert on chimpanzees. She began traveling widely. Thousands of people all around the world read her book *In the Shadow of Man*. They were fascinated by her stories about David Graybeard, Flo, Mr. McGregor, and Goblin. Jane visited many schools, where kids nicknamed her the Chimp Lady. They yelled "Yuck!" when she told them how she sampled the foods chimps ate—including termites, which she thought were rather bland.

Jane taught occasionally at Stanford University in California, and she often spoke at scientific meetings in the United States, Canada, and Europe. Her favorite trips, though, were visiting African parks with Grub and Derek, who at that time was the director of Tanzania's national park system.

Jane and Derek shared many happy times, but tragedy lay ahead. Cancer struck Derek. In October 1980, he lost his battle with the disease. Grief-stricken for the man she called the love of her life, Jane visited her family briefly at the Birches in England. Then she returned to Derek's house in Dar es Salaam.

She healed the most when she went to Gombe—not to record her observations, but to find peace by herself, among the chimps she loved. As Jane's spirit revived, she devoted more of her time to writing books and traveling worldwide to raise money to help chimps. Grub attended school in England, spending his holidays with Jane or his father.

Jane established the Jane Goodall Institute for Wildlife Research, Education, and Conservation now located in Ridgefield, Connecticut. This organization raises funds to protect chimpanzees all across Africa. With researchers from local villages working at Gombe, the chimps there are safe. However, the number of wild chimps living elsewhere in Africa has decreased rapidly.

In 1900, chimps were common throughout the African continent. Hundreds of thousands of them lived in twenty-five nations. Today, only five countries have major chimp populations, and their numbers are decreasing. Most females are nowhere near as successful as Flo in raising many youngsters. The average chimp mother raises only two infants in her lifetime. If chimp communities were left alone, they would remain relatively stable in size. However, humans do not leave the chimps alone.

Unlike chimp mothers, women often have many children, especially in poor countries. As the human population soars, forests where chimps live are cut down to make room for houses and farms. The Gombe Stream Reserve, now a national park, used to be surrounded by miles of lush forests, but today the bordering trees are gone. The lake and streams are becoming polluted.

Chimps in unprotected areas have almost nowhere to live. In addition, human starvation has led to the hunting of chimps, sometimes for food and sometimes to be sold.

Some infant chimps are captured to be sold as pets. Usually the mother is shot, and the infant's hands and feet are tied together. The young chimp is placed in a small box or basket and taken to a dealer's camp. Thirsty and hungry, chimps who do not die within a few days of capture become emotional cripples longing for their mothers and families. Because such trading is illegal, a chimp infant smuggled overseas is usually put into a box that won't be recognized as a container with a small animal hidden in it. The chimp orphans are completely isolated, and as many die of loneliness as of starvation. It has been estimated that at least ten chimps die for every one that survives to reach its destination.

Jane is trying to get African governments to seize chimps offered for sale at markets. If the chimps are bought, traders are encouraged to kill more mothers and sell their babies for a profit. But if governments can enforce their laws by taking the chimps away from poachers before the animals are sold, perhaps the cruelty can be stopped. If turned loose, the captured infants would quickly die without the love and protection of their mothers. Jane's institute has set up safe places for chimp orphans to grow up where trained workers give them love, attention, and healthy food in a natural environment.

Sometimes well-meaning people buy young chimps at the market because they feel sorry for them. They try to care for the cuddly chimps like human children. At first the chimps make cute little playmates. But by the time the chimps are six years old, they are young adolescents as strong as a human adult. They are dangerous. What is a family to do with a chimp that bites, hurls objects in anger, leaps around the room, and intimidates its "superiors"? Owners have been known to have the chimps' teeth pulled out, or even cut off the animals' thumbs so they can't grip things. Sometimes a chimp may be put in a tiny cage where it "won't make any trouble." But full-grown chimps almost always must be removed from households.

If they are sent to zoos, chimps raised in a human home become outcasts. They have not learned how to

Photo by Steve Matthews. Courtesy of the Jane Goodall Institute.

Jane hugs Whiskey, a chimp who lived chained in his owner's garage since the age of six. Jane has become a tireless crusader for compassionate and humane treatment of captive chimps.

behave within a chimp community, so they do not fit in. Jane discovered an adult chimp named Gregoire who had spent years caged alone at a zoo in the Congo. Skinny, hairless, and staring vacantly ahead, he reminded Jane of human victims of World War II concentration camps.

The entertainment industry still buys chimps, and Jane has found that many of them are abused. She has seen chimps dressed in human clothes who were beaten and drugged until they were so unnaturally calm that they allowed tourists to pick them up to be photographed together. Jane found one such chimp in the Canary Islands. She uttered chimp sounds to the animal, who seemed so reassured by the familiar noises that he clung to her neck, refusing to let her go.

Some chimps become performers in circuses or movies. Training animals with love and positive feedback takes more time than a trainer may be willing to give. It's quicker to use force, so some chimp "stars" have been beaten cruelly with iron bars or given electric shocks. Viewers watching a cute chimp perform tricks rarely have any idea what brutal treatment the animal may have suffered to learn such behavior. By means of a radio-controlled unit strapped to the chimp's back, a trainer can give an electric shock to a chimp who "misbehaves." A chimp's mouth may be wired shut during performances.

Chimps are so much like people that chimps' basic genetic material is almost ninety-nine percent the same as that of humans. If the blood type is matched, a human and a chimp could even have a transfusion from each other. Because of these biological similarities, medical researchers use chimps to study human diseases. Chimps are deliberately infected with the AIDS virus, hepatitis, or other deadly diseases so researchers can learn more about possible treatments. Jane has said she will be haunted forever by the eyes of some of the chimps she has visited in medical labs. Sluggish, lonely, and depressed, the young animals have given up on life—if their existence in isolated, tiny cages could be called life at all.

Human suffering will be greatly reduced when cures for deadly diseases are found, but Jane points out that the conditions in the labs make the chimps' suffering far worse than necessary to meet the research goals. She urges that the chimps be given toys, be allowed to go outdoors, have more contact with each other, and be housed in larger cages.

Chimps in some modern zoos may live in the best conditions of all captive chimps, but many zoos still cram animals together in cement cells. Bored, frustrated, and emotionally disabled, such chimps could have much better lives if the zookeepers better understood the animals' needs. The Jane Goodall Institute funds the study of chimpanzees living in zoos. As a result of the research, students, zookeepers, and volunteers have done a great deal to improve the living conditions for many chimps in captivity—giving them more varied food, larger enclosures, and more things to do.

Jane regularly leaves her beloved chimps at Gombe so that she can help all chimps. Talking to groups of people, she shows slides of Flo and her family, Goliath and Goblin, Figan and Fifi. In her soft voice and slight British accent, she speaks movingly about the animals she loves. She is determined to save their environment in Africa and to improve conditions for chimps everywhere.

"I've learned so much from observing chimpanzees," she says. "I feel it's my responsibility to give them something back."

Often she tells the story of a chimp called Old Man. Jane guesses that he may have been in a lab or a circus before a zoo in North America bought him as an adolescent. Old Man hated people. The zoo put him on an island with three adult females. He fathered a baby chimp just about the same time that the zoo hired a new keeper named Marc. Marc was warned that the chimps were dangerous, so he fed them by throwing food to the island from his boat.

After a while Marc started talking to the chimps from the boat, and one day Old Man accepted a banana from Marc's hand. Next Marc came onto the island. The female chimps were hostile toward him, but Marc was able to make friends with Old Man.

One day Marc slipped and fell near the infant chimp, who screamed in fright. The mother jumped up to protect her baby. She bit Marc's neck, and the other two females joined in attacking him. They bit his arm and leg. Blood poured from his wounds. Then Old Man grabbed the females one by one and pulled them away from Marc. Badly hurt, Marc dragged himself toward the boat. Old Man stood close by, scaring the females away. Marc says there is no doubt that Old Man saved his life.

After telling about Marc and Old Man, Jane says, "If a chimpanzee can reach out to help a human, then we humans can reach out and try to help the chimpanzees and all the other creatures we live with in the world today. This is what I am trying to do. I hope you will help me."

For Further Reading

Books by Jane Goodall

The Chimpanzee Family Book. Saxonville, MA: Picture Book Studio, 1991.

Grub, the Bush Baby. (Hugo van Lawick, coauthor.) Boston: Houghton Mifflin, 1988.

Jane Goodall's Animal World: Elephants. New York: Aladdin, 1990.

Jane Goodall's Animal World: Gorillas. New York: Aladdin, 1990.

Jane Goodall's Animal World: Sea Otters. New York: Aladdin, 1990.

Jane Goodall's Animal World: Tigers. New York: Aladdin, 1990.

My Life with the Chimpanzees. New York: Pocket Books, 1988.

With Love. Ridgefield, CT: Jane Goodall Institute, 1994.

Books About Jane Goodall

Fromer, Julie. *Jane Goodall: Living with the Chimps.* New York: Twenty-first Century Books, 1992.

Lucas, Eileen. *Jane Goodall: Friend of the Chimps.* Brookfield, CT: Millbrook Press, 1992.

Senn, J. A. *Jane Goodall, Naturalist.* Woodbridge, CT: Blackbirch Press, 1993.

Index